Easy Piano

# glee

## Music From The FOX Television Show

ISBN 978-1-4234-7727-3

HAL•LEONARD®
CORPORATION
7777 W. BLUEMOUND RD. P.O. BOX 13819 MILWAUKEE, WI 53213

Visit Hal Leonard Online at
**www.halleonard.com**

# ALONE

Words and Music by BILLY STEINBERG
and TOM KELLY

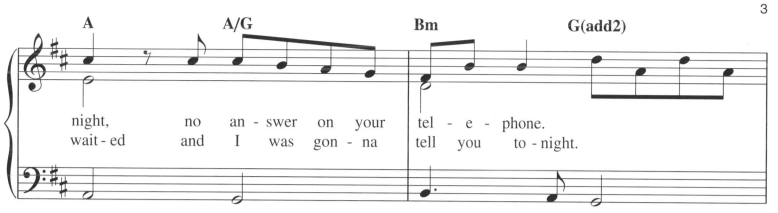

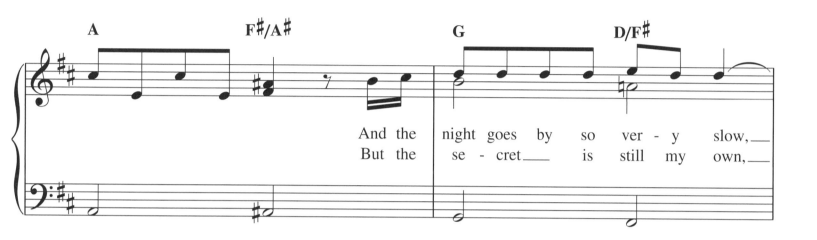

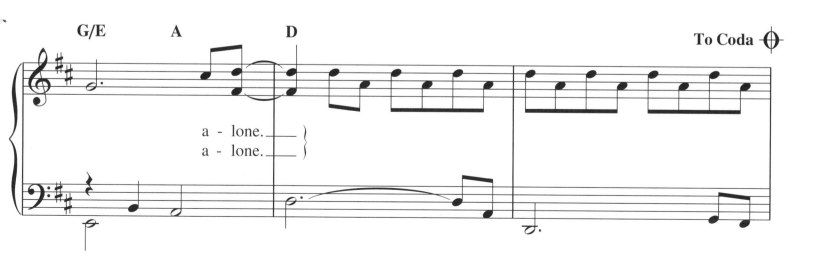

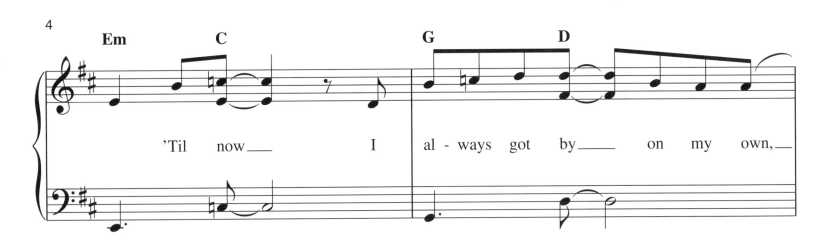

'Til now___ I al - ways got by___ on my own,___

___ I nev - er real - ly cared un - til I met you. And now it

chills me to the bone. How do I get___ you a - lone?___

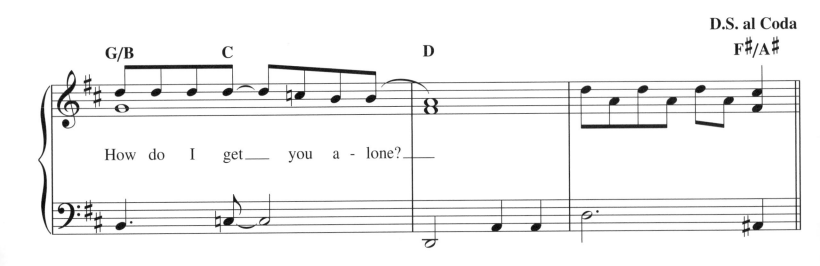

D.S. al Coda

How do I get___ you a - lone?___

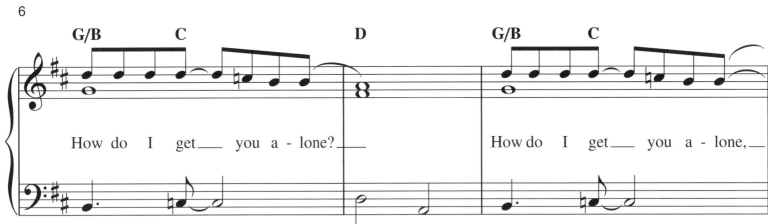

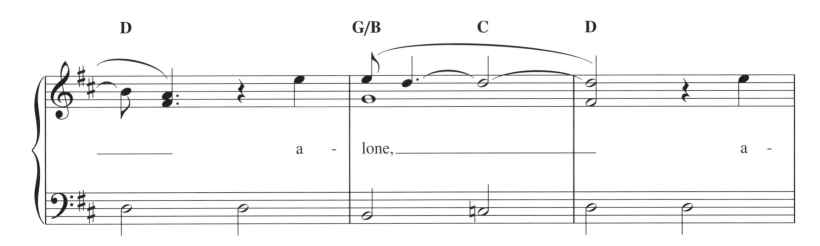

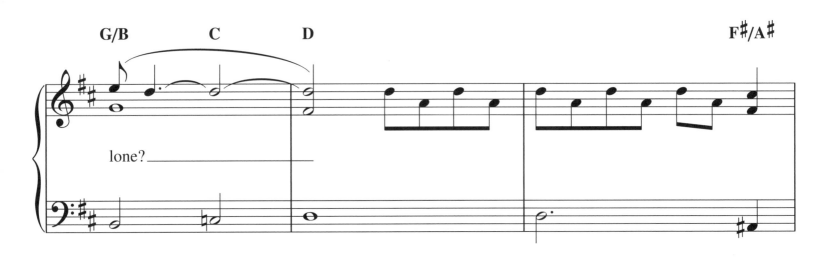

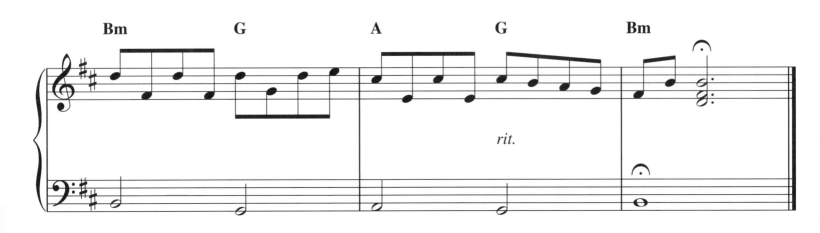

How do I get___ you a-lone?___ How do I get___ you a-lone,___

a - lone,_____ a -

lone?_____

rit.

# DON'T RAIN ON MY PARADE

**from FUNNY GIRL**

Words by BOB MERRILL
Music by JULE STYNE

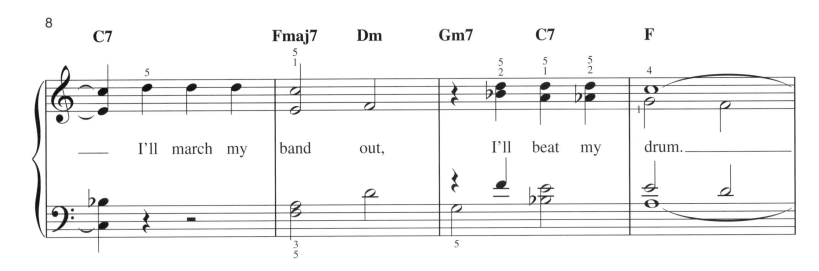

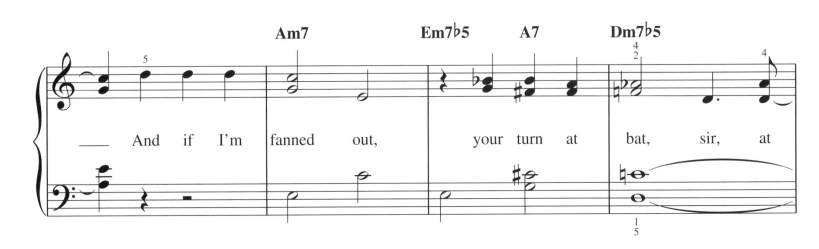

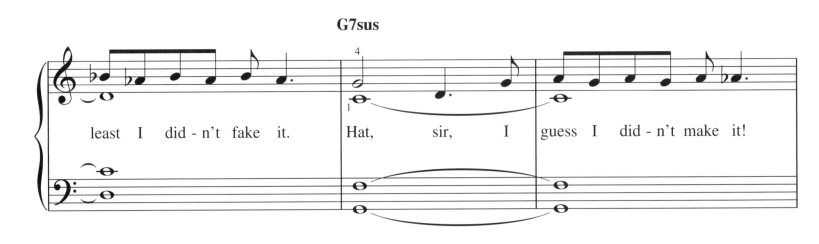

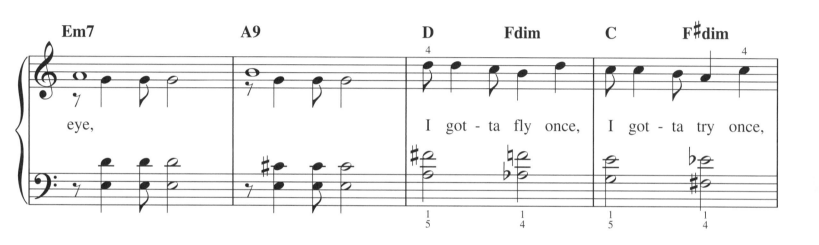

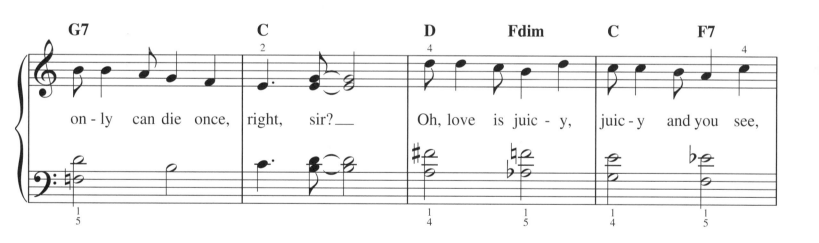

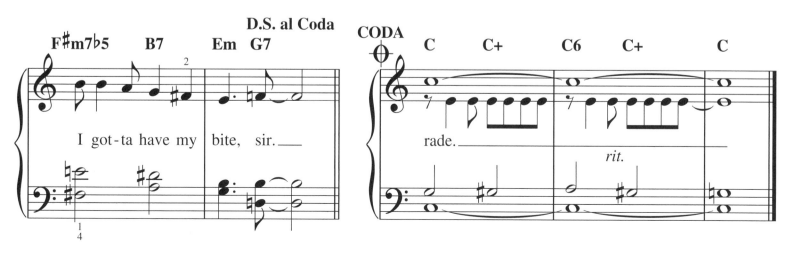

# DEFYING GRAVITY
### from the Broadway Musical WICKED

Music and Lyrics by
STEPHEN SCHWARTZ

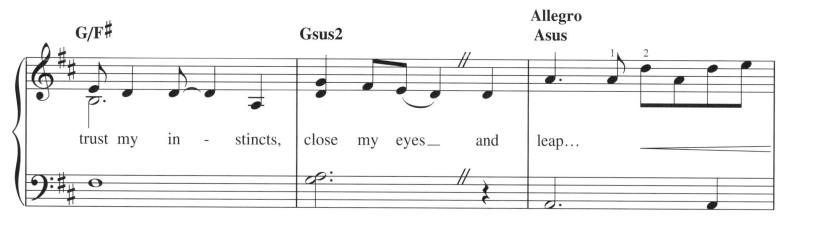

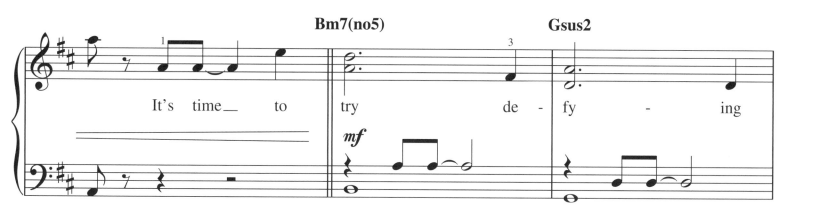

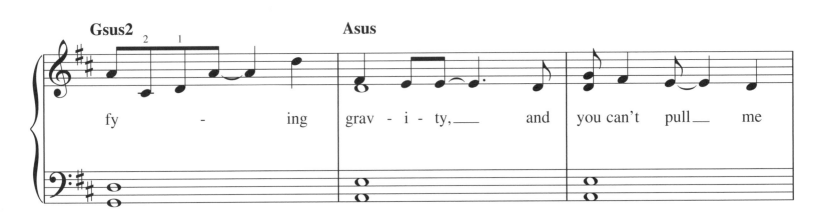

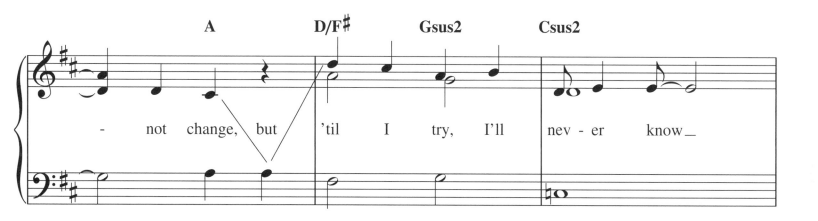

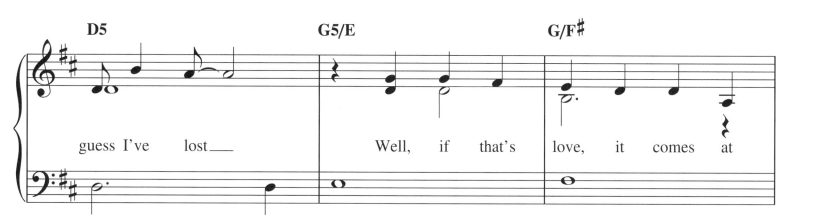

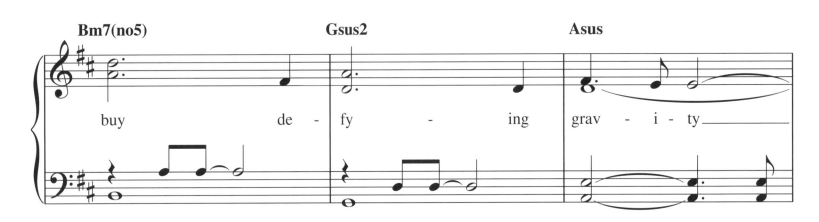

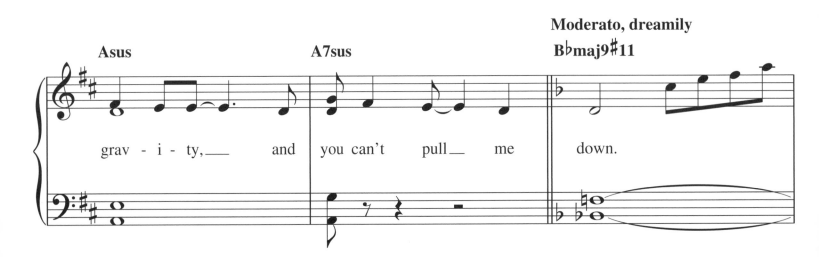

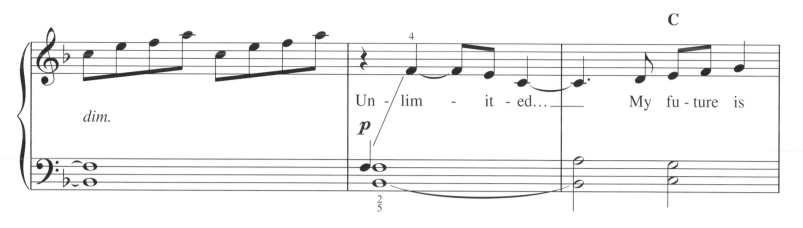

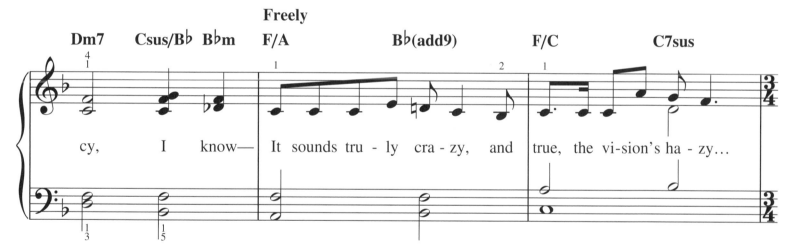

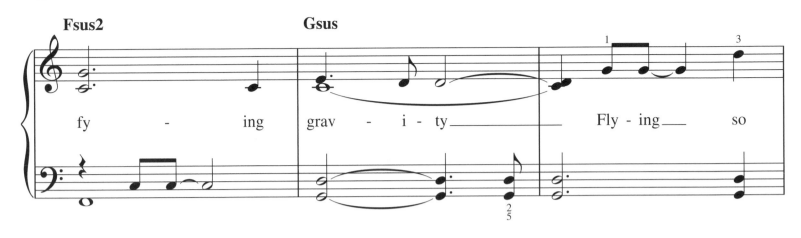

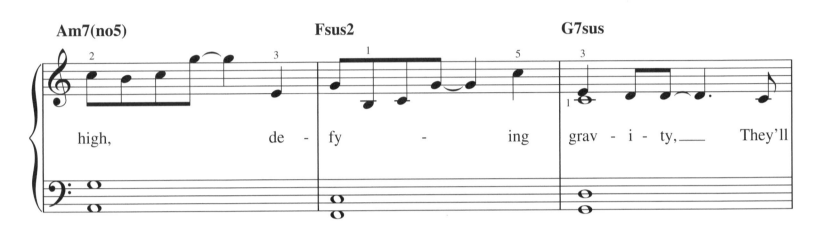

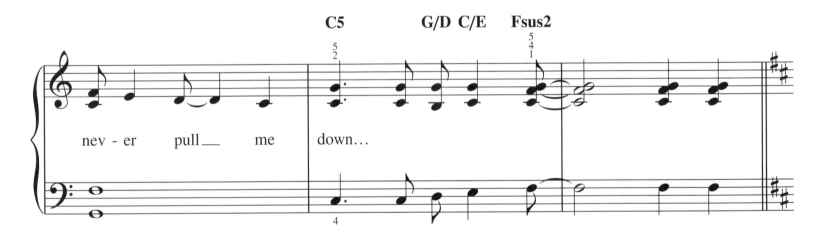

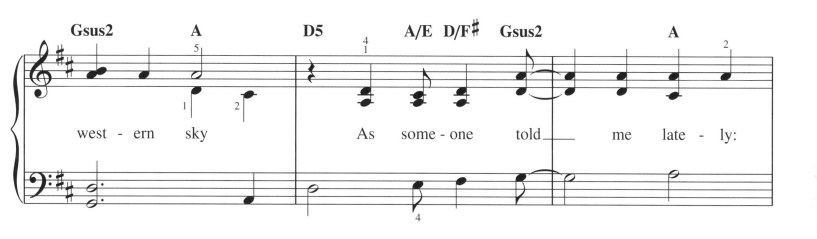

ground me, take a mes-sage back— from me…

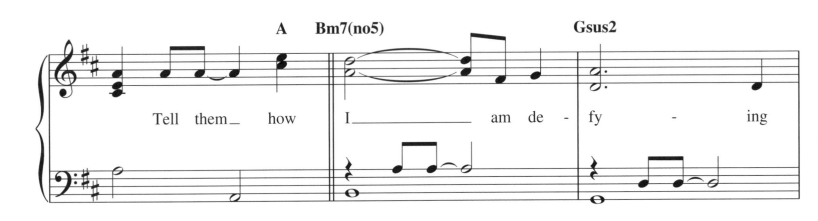

Tell them— how I_____ am de - fy - ing

grav - i - ty_____ I'm fly - ing high de -

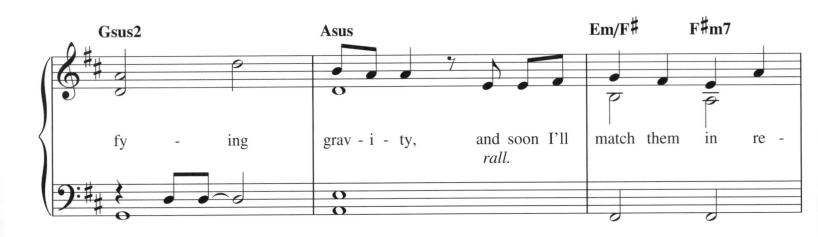

fy - ing grav - i - ty, and soon I'll match them in re -

*rall.*

**With determination, slower**

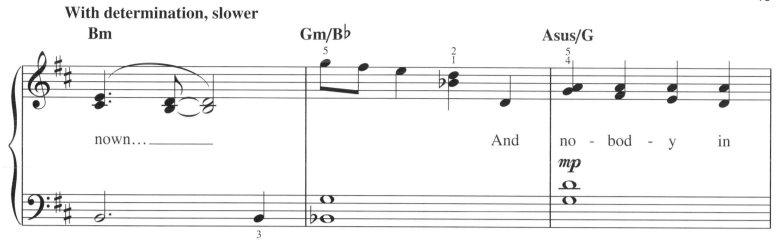

nown… And no - bod - y in

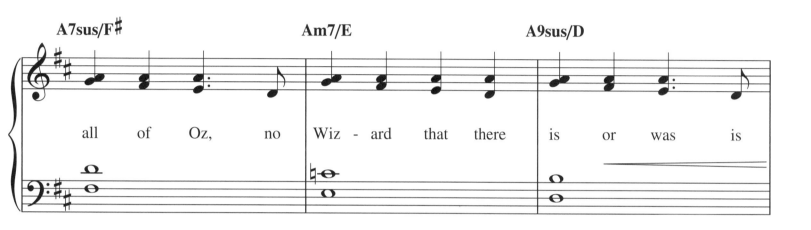

all of Oz, no Wiz - ard that there is or was is

ev - er gon - na bring me down…

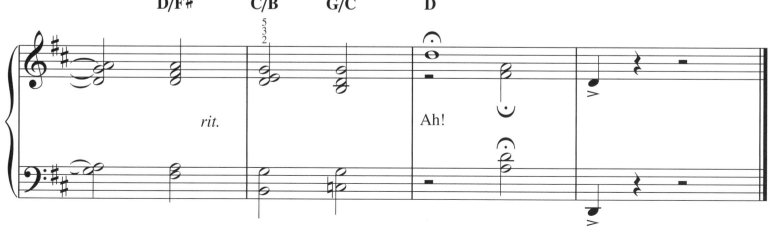

*rit.* Ah!

# DON'T STOP BELIEVIN'

Words and Music by STEVE PERRY,
NEAL SCHON and JONATHAN CAIN

small-town girl, \_\_\_\_
cit - y boy, \_\_\_\_

Just a
Just a

liv - in' in a
born and raised in

lone - ly world. _____
south De - troit. _____

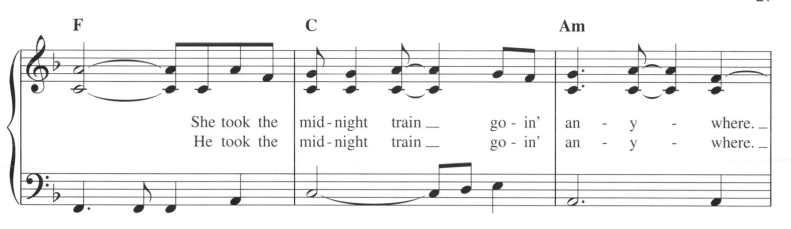

She took the mid-night train __ go - in' an - y - where. __
He took the mid-night train __ go - in' an - y - where. __

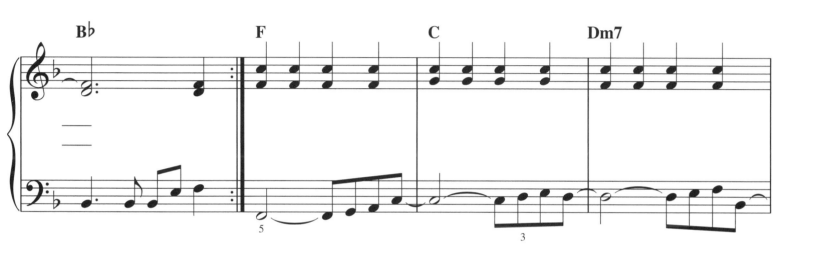

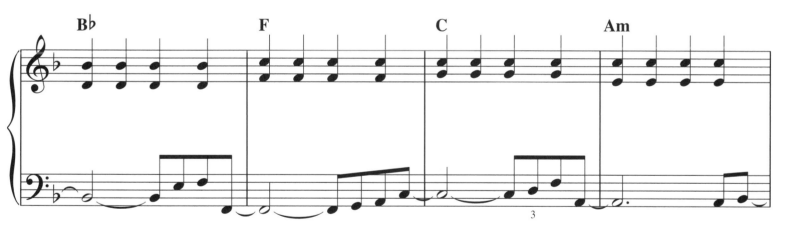

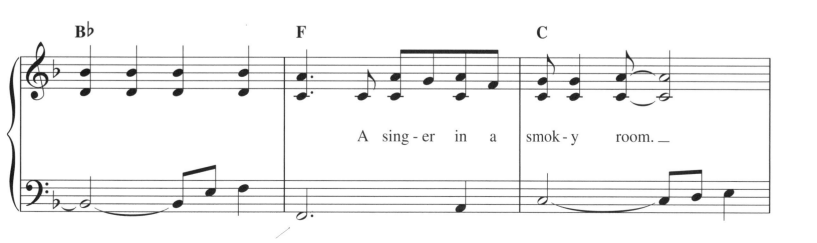

A sing - er in a smok - y room. __

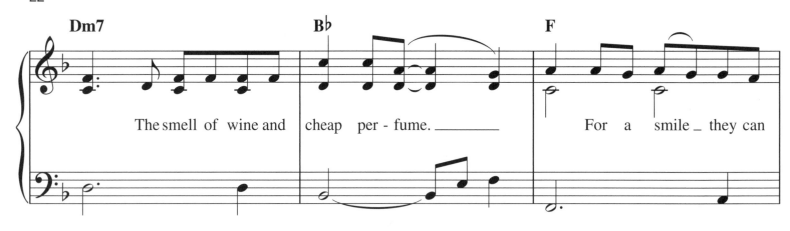

The smell of wine and cheap per - fume. _____ For a smile __ they can

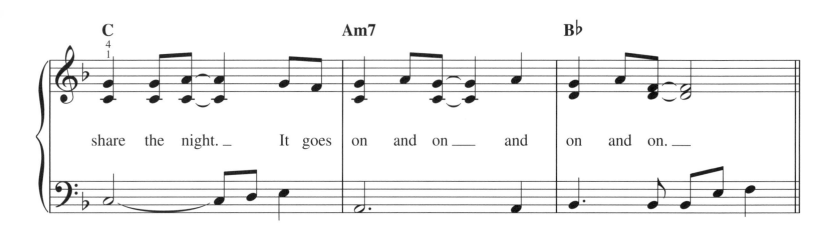

share the night. __ It goes on and on ___ and on and on. ___

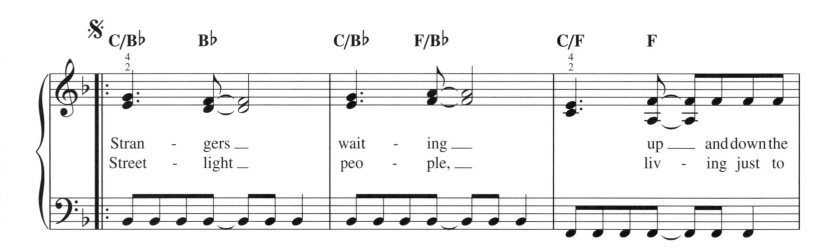

Stran - gers ___ wait - ing ___ up ___ and down the

Street - light ___ peo - ple, ___ liv - ing just to

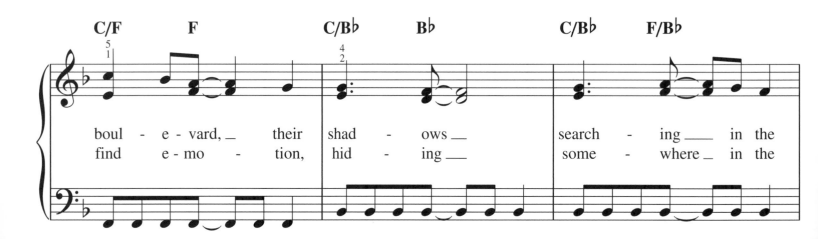

boul - e - vard, __ their shad - ows ___ search - ing ___ in the

find e - mo - tion, hid - ing ___ some - where __ in the

**D.S. al Coda (with repeat)**

**CODA**

2. | Am7 — on and on ___ and | Bb — on and on. ___

F — Don't _ stop _ be-

C — liev - in'. ___

Dm7 — Hold on to the feel - in', _____

Bb

F — street - light ___

C — peo - ple. ___

Am

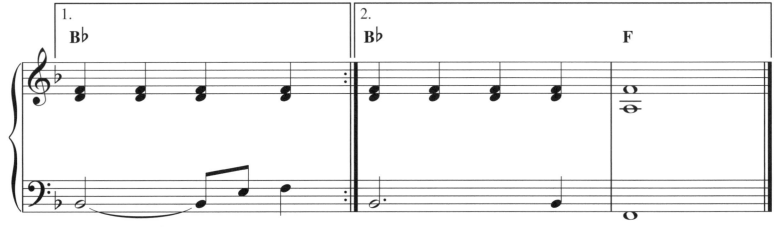

1. | Bb

2. | Bb

F

# I'LL STAND BY YOU

Words and Music by CHRISSIE HYNDE,
TOM KELLY and BILLY STEINBERG

When the night falls on you, you don't know what to do. Noth-ing you con-

fess could make me love you less.____ I'll stand by you, I'll stand by

you,____ won't let no-bod-y hurt you,____ I'll stand by you.

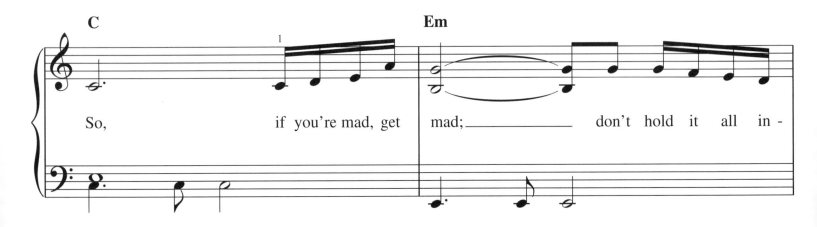

So, if you're mad, get mad;____ don't hold it all in-

side._____ Come on and talk to me now. And hey, what you got to

hide? I get an-gry, too, well, I'm a lot like you. When you're

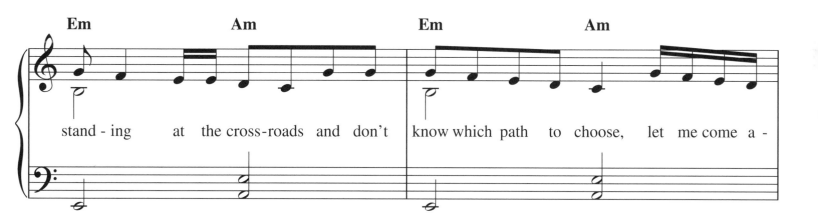

stand - ing at the cross-roads and don't know which path to choose, let me come a -

long, 'cause e-ven if you're wrong,_____ I'll stand by you. I'll stand by

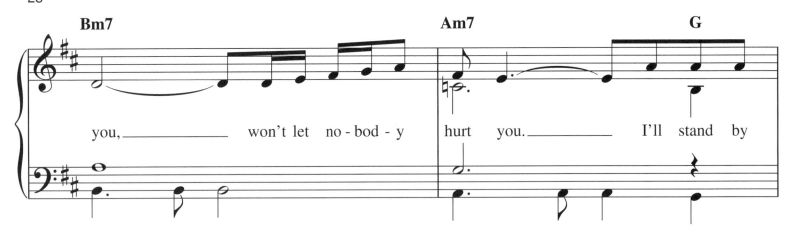

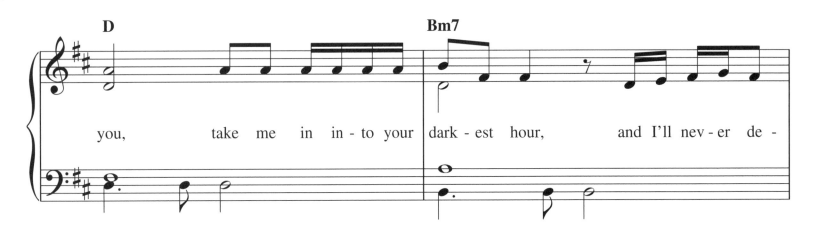

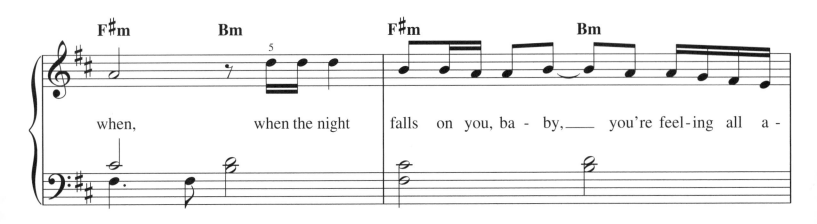

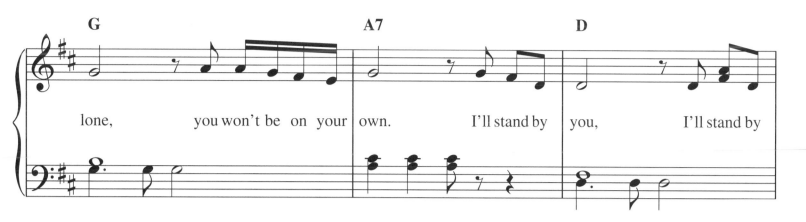

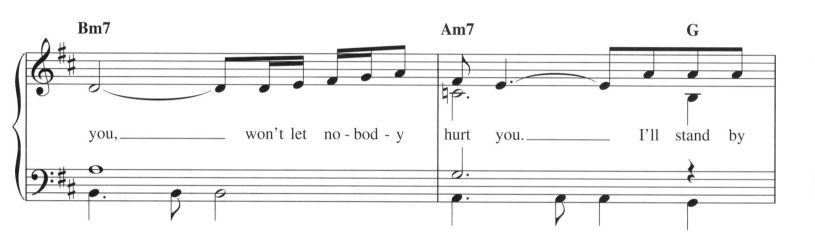

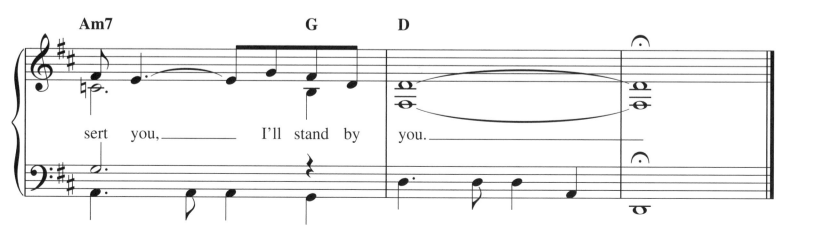

# IMAGINE

Words and Music by
JOHN LENNON

**Slowly**

(Sheet music, first system)

Chords: C — Cmaj7 — F — C — Cmaj7

(Second system)

Chords: F — C — Cmaj7

I - mag - ine there's    no   heav -
I - mag - ine there's    no   coun -
I - mag - ine   no   pos - ses -

(Third system)

Chords: F — C — Cmaj7

en.      It's   eas - y   if   you      try.
tries.   It   is - n't   hard   to      do.
sions.   I   won - der   if   you      can.

(Fourth system)

Chords: F — C — Cmaj7 — F

No   hell    be - low    us,
Noth - ing   to   kill   or   die   for
No   need   for   greed   or   hun - ger,

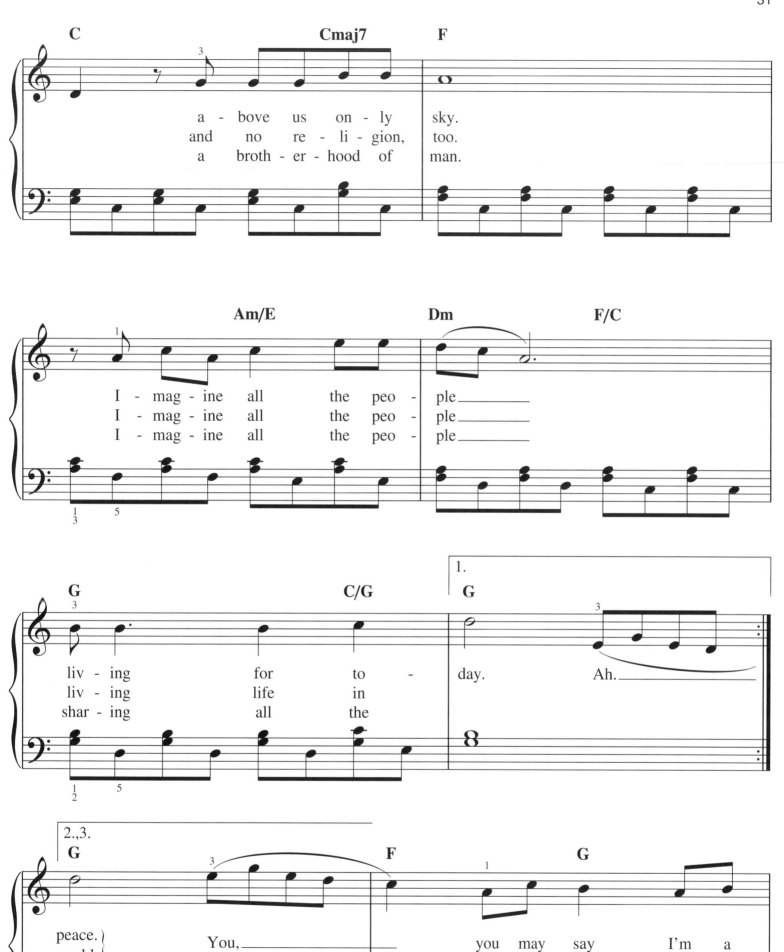

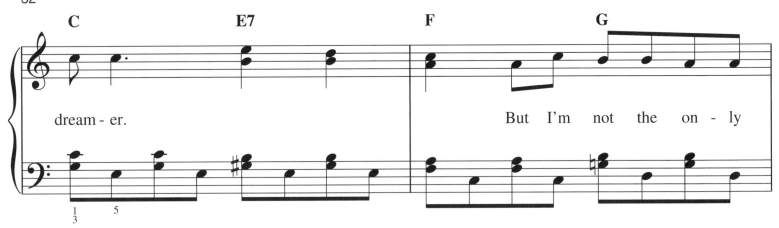

dream - er.　　　　　　　　But I'm not the on - ly

one.　　　　　　　　I hope some - day_____ you'll

To Coda $\oplus$　　　　　　　　D.S. al Coda
(take 2nd ending)

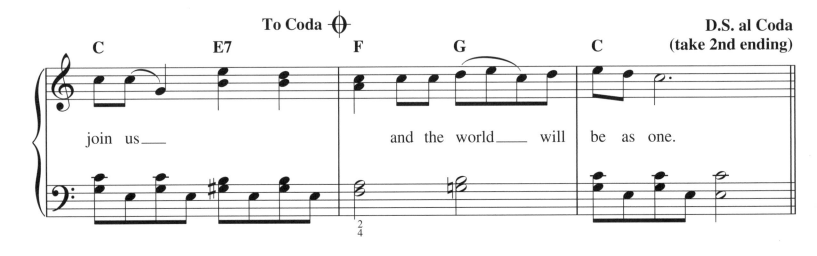

join us___　　　　　and the world___ will　be as one.

CODA

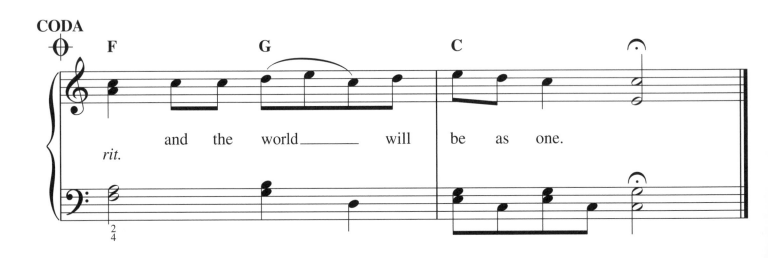

rit.　and the world_____ will　be as one.

# KEEP HOLDING ON

from the Twentieth Century Fox Motion Picture ERAGON

Words and Music by AVRIL LAVIGNE
and LUKASZ GOTTWALD

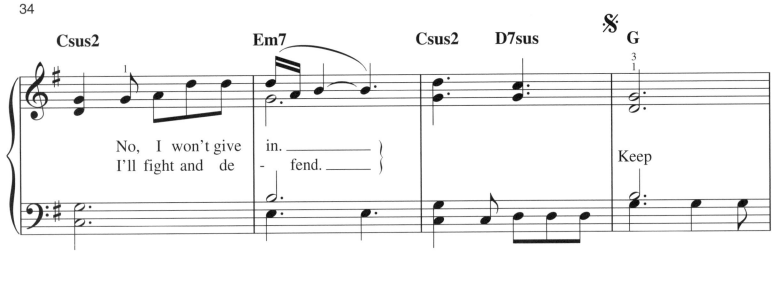

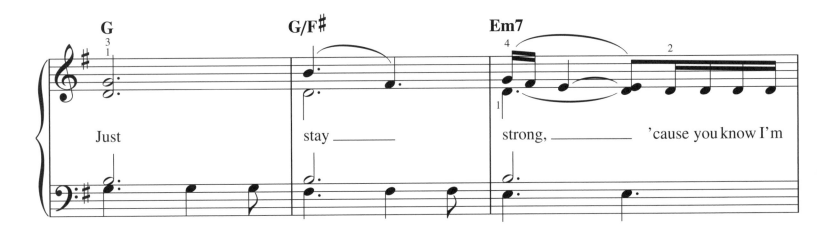

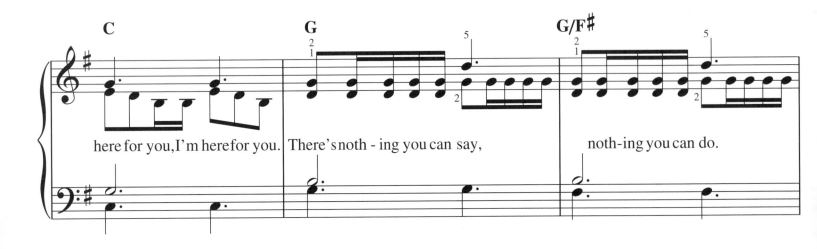

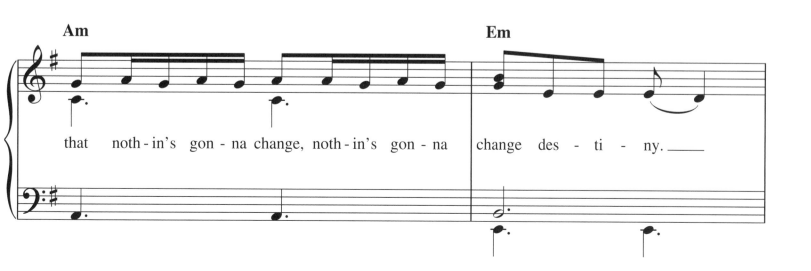

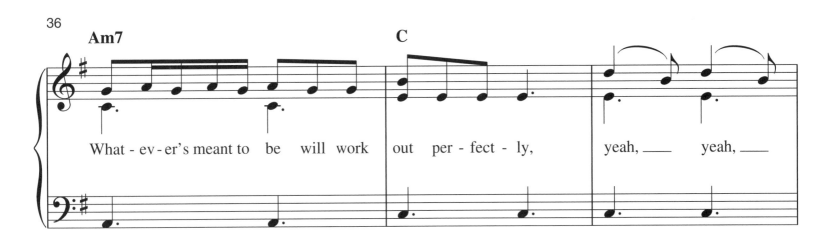

What - ev - er's meant to be will work out per - fect - ly, yeah, _____ yeah, _____

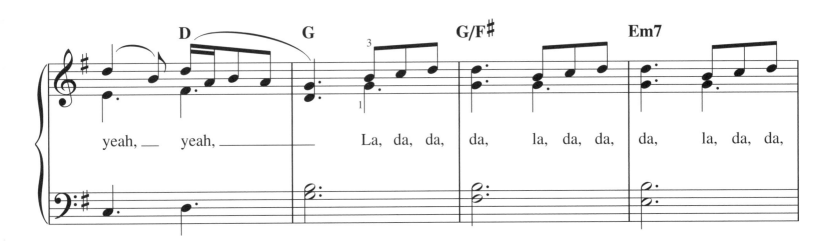

yeah, _____ yeah, _____ La, da, da, da, la, da, da, da, la, da, da,

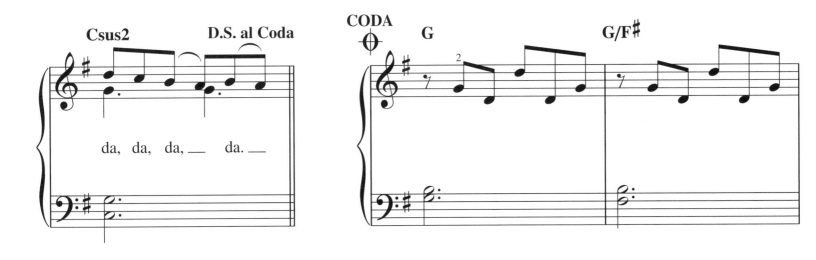

da, da, da, _____ da. _____

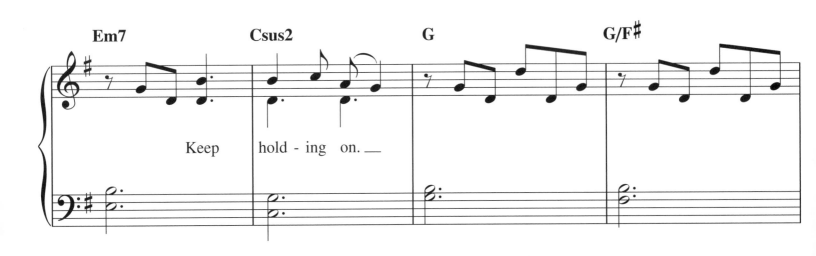

Keep hold - ing on. _____

# LEAN ON ME

Words and Music by
BILL WITHERS

**Moderately**

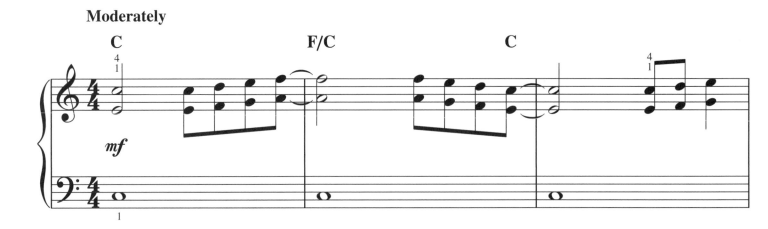

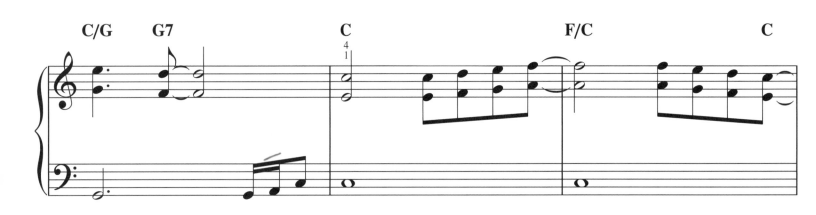

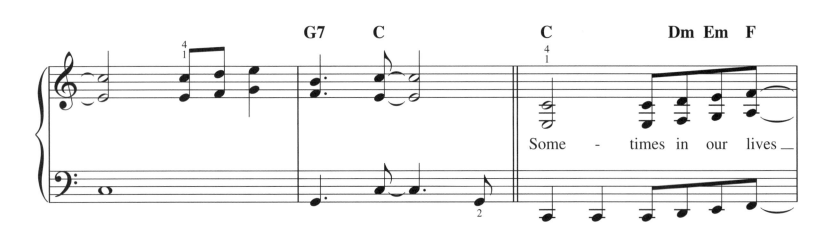

Some - times in our lives ___

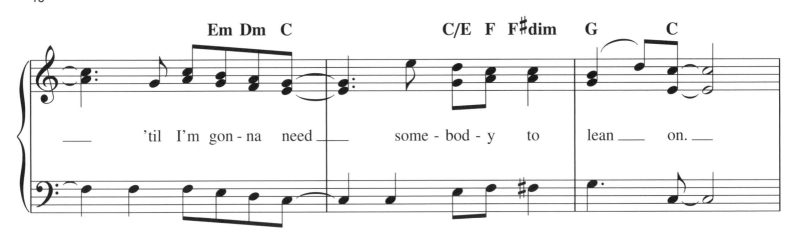

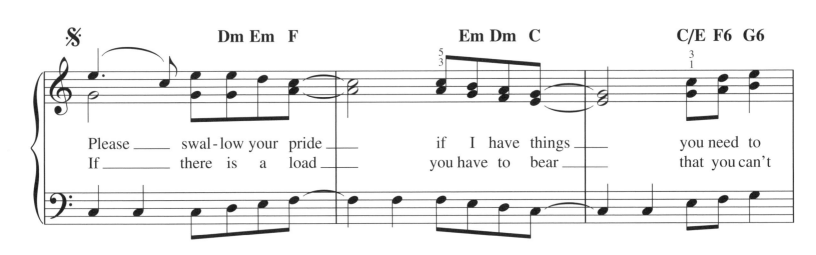

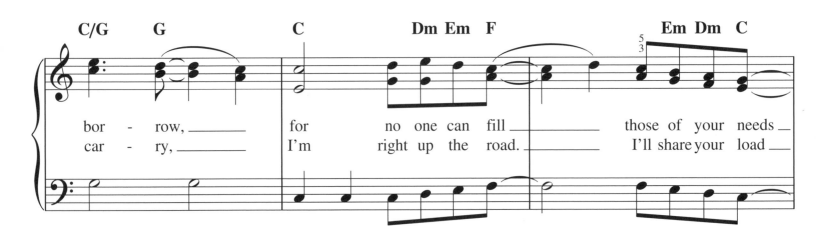

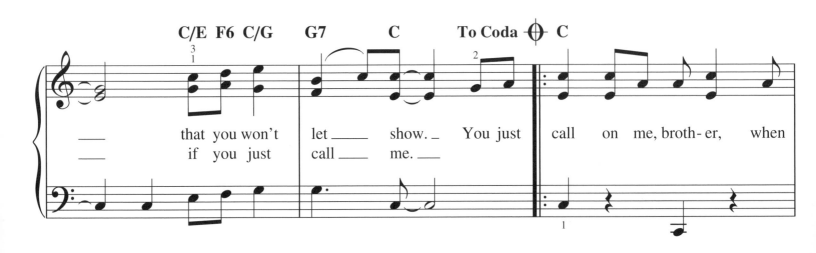

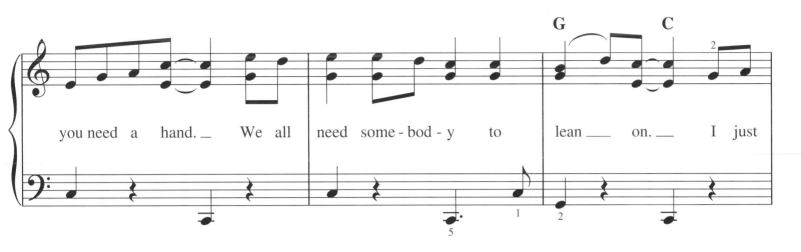

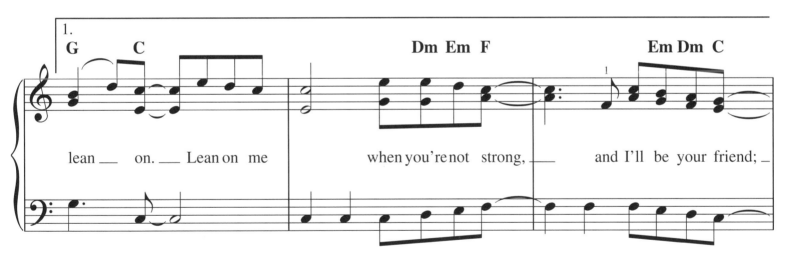

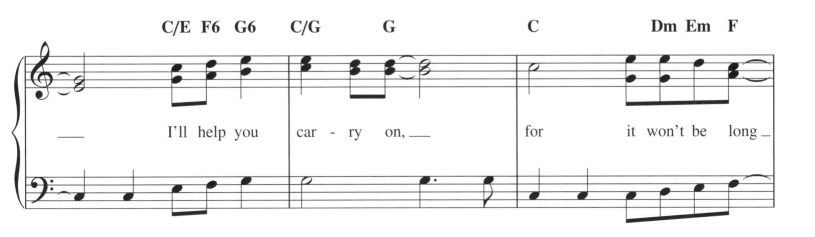

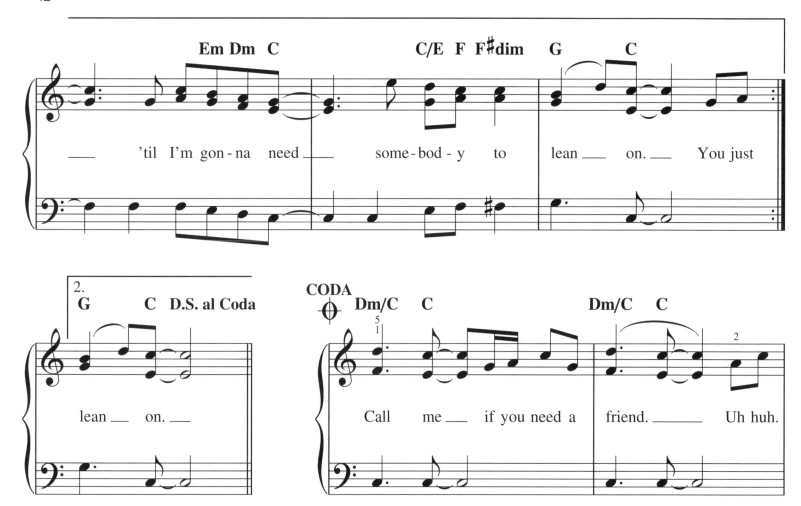

**Em Dm C**        **C/E F F♯dim**   **G**      **C**

_____ 'til I'm gon - na need _____ some - bod - y to lean _____ on. _____ You just

**2.**
**G**      **C D.S. al Coda**

lean _____ on. _____

**CODA**    **Dm/C**    **C**          **Dm/C**   **C**

Call me _____ if you need a friend. _____ Uh huh.

**Dm/C**      **C**        **Dm/C**    **C**        **Dm/C**    **C**

Call me _____ if you need a friend. _____ Uh huh. Call me. _____

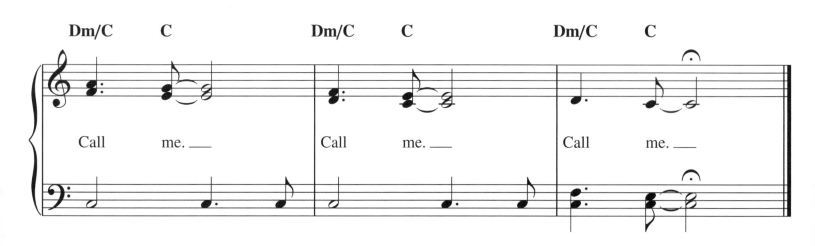

**Dm/C**      **C**        **Dm/C**    **C**        **Dm/C**    **C**

Call me. _____ Call me. _____ Call me. _____

# NO AIR

Words and Music by JAMES FAUNTLEROY II,
STEVEN RUSSELL, HARVEY MASON JR.,
DAMON THOMAS and ERIK GRIGGS

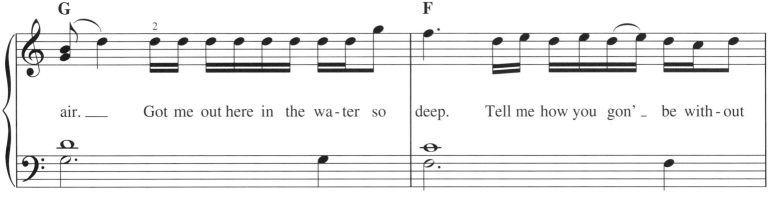

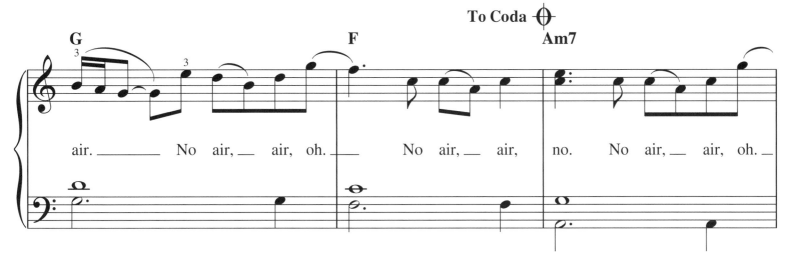

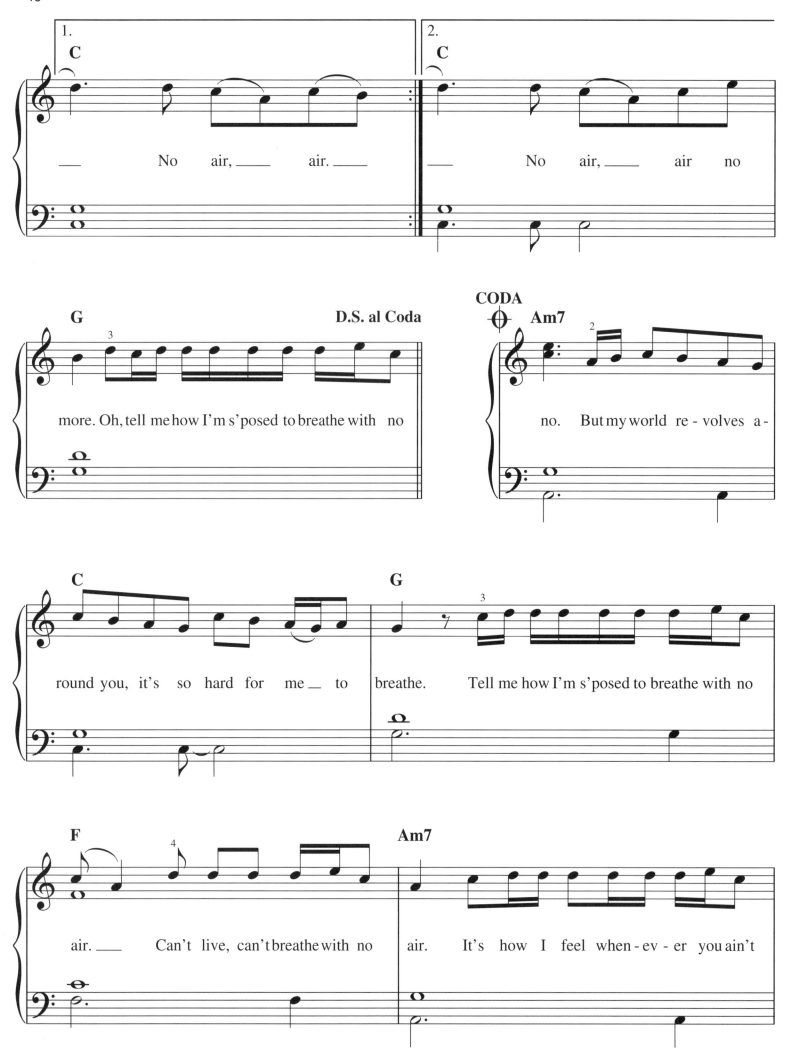

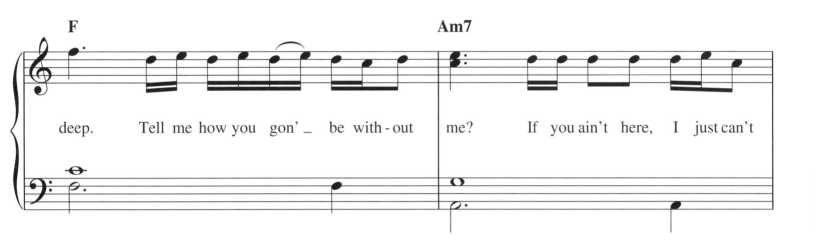

# MY LIFE WOULD SUCK WITHOUT YOU

Words and Music by LUKASZ GOTTWALD,
MAX MARTIN and CLAUDE KELLY

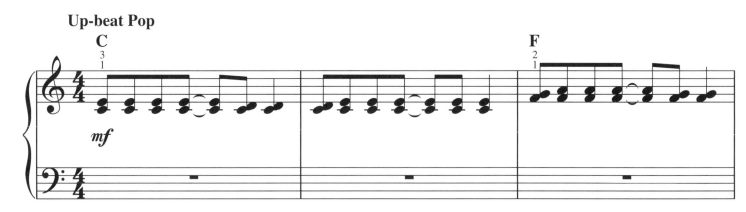

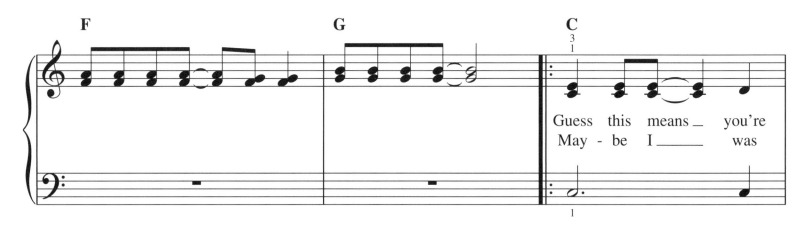

Guess this means ___ you're
May - be I ____ was

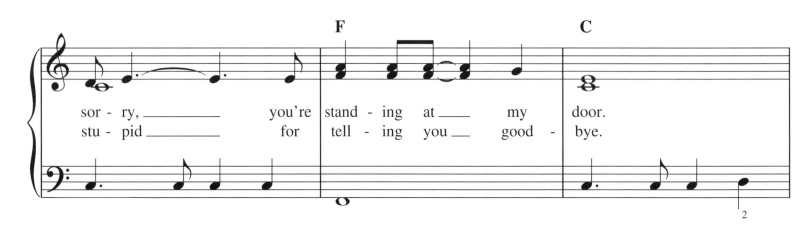

sor - ry, _____ you're stand - ing at ___ my door.
stu - pid _____ for tell - ing you ___ good - bye.

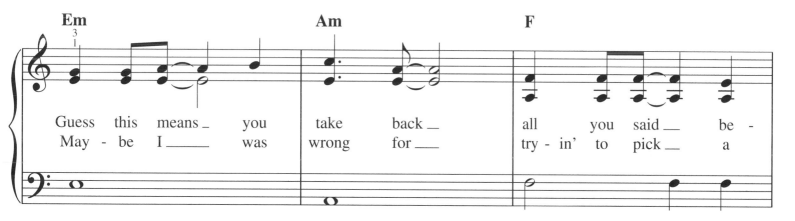

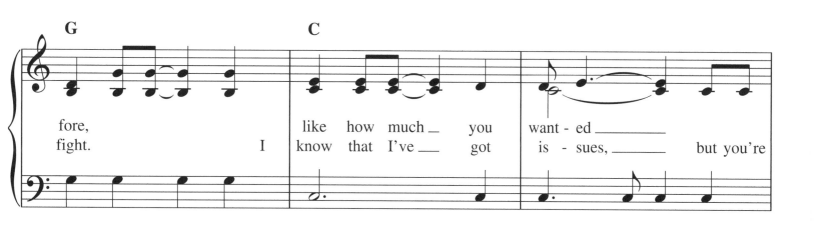

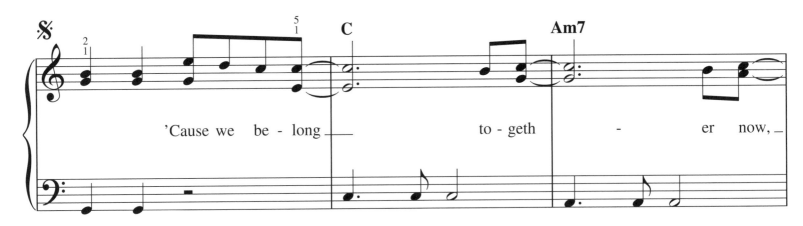

'Cause we be-long _____ to-geth - er now, _____

_____ yeah, for-ev-er u - nit - ed here _____

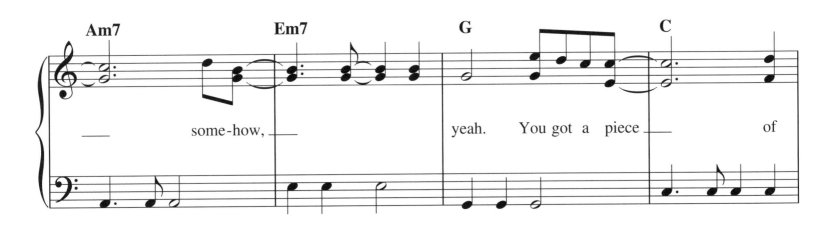

_____ some-how, _____ yeah. You got a piece _____ of

me. And hon-est - ly, my

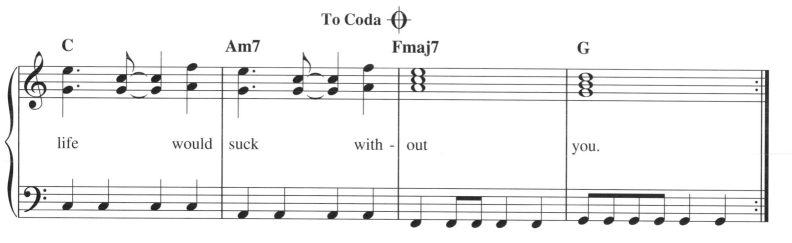

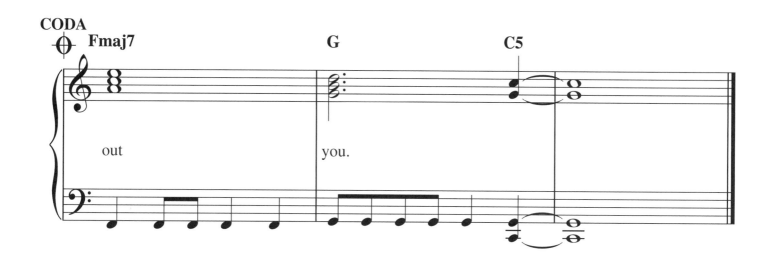

# SOMEBODY TO LOVE

Words and Music by
FREDDIE MERCURY

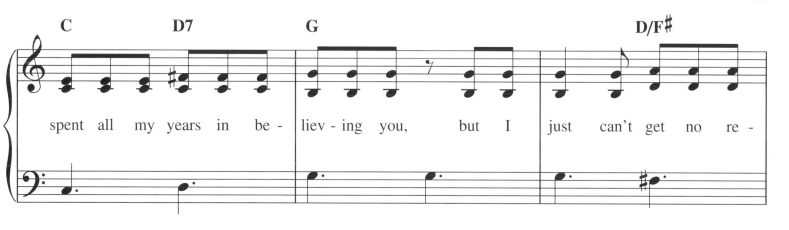

spent all my years in be - liev - ing you, but I just can't get no re -

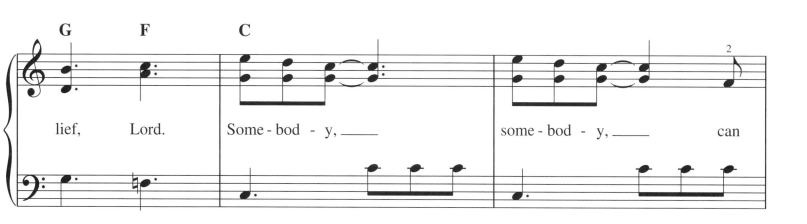

lief, Lord. Some - bod - y, _____ some - bod - y, _____ can

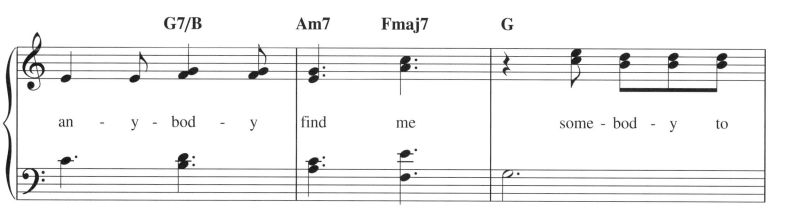

an - y - bod - y find me some - bod - y to

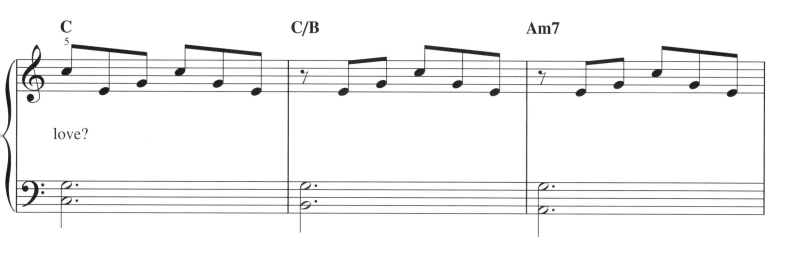

love?

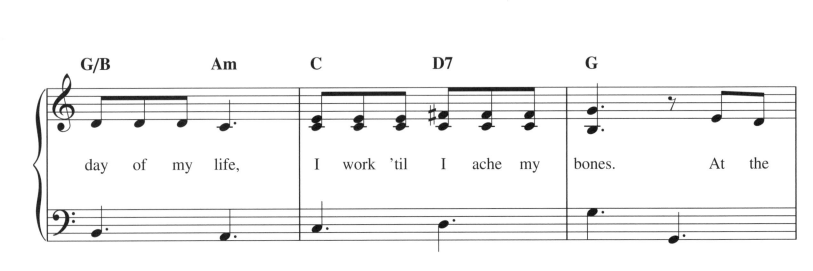

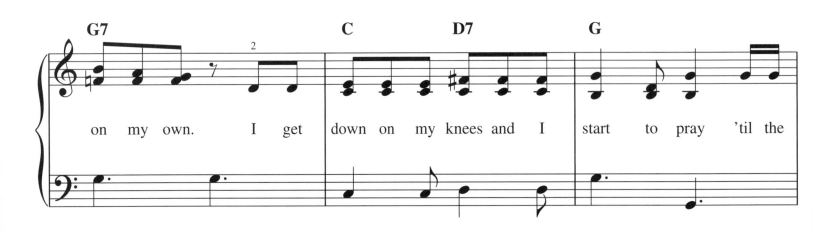

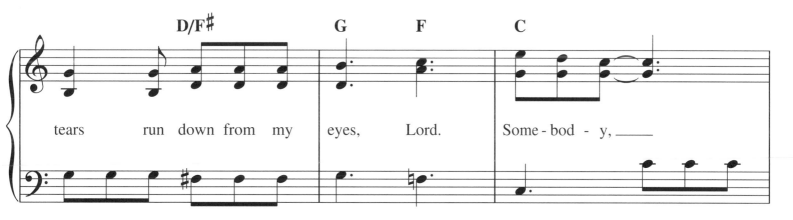

tears    run down from my    eyes,    Lord.    Some - bod - y, _____

some - bod - y, _____    can    an - y - bod - y    find    me

some - bod - y to    love?

Ev - 'ry _____

day      I    try    and I   try    and I     try, _____ but

ev -    'ry - bod - y    wants   to    put   me   down, they    say    I'm   go - in'

cra -   zy. \_\_\_\_ They    say   I    got   a   lot   of   wat - er   in   my    brain, _____

got   no   com - mon   sense. I   got    no - bod - y   left     to   be -    lieve. _____

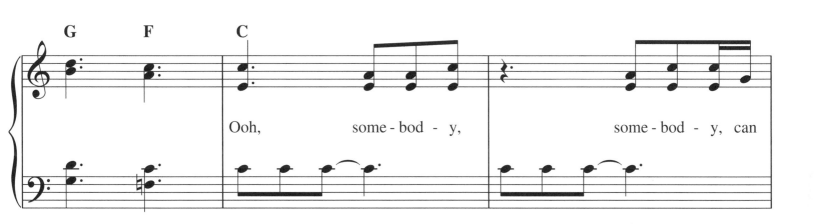

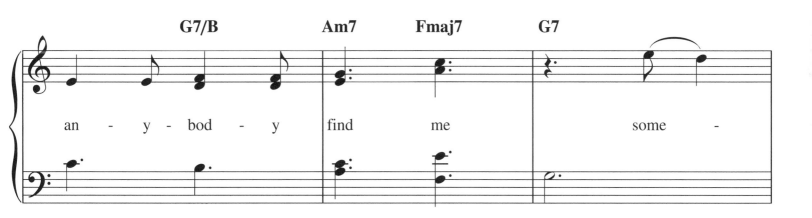

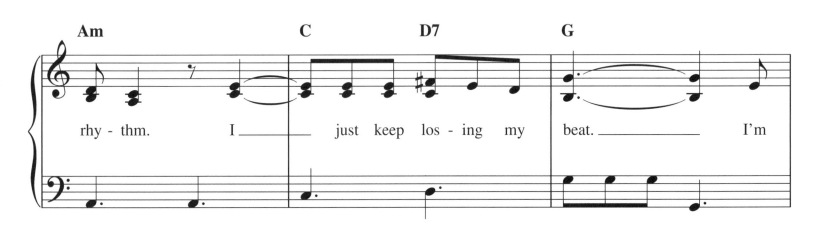

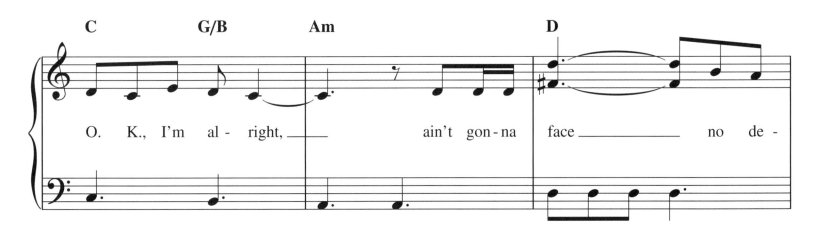

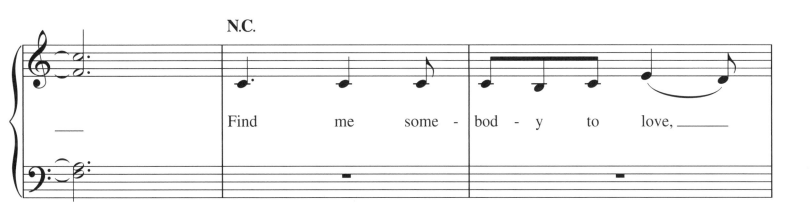

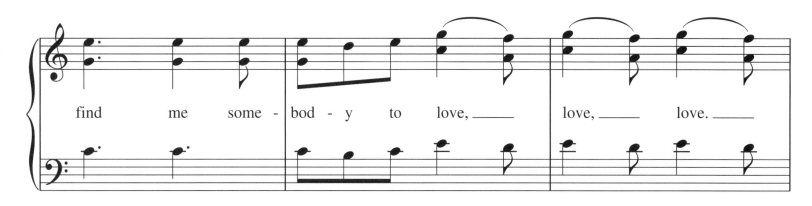

find me some - bod - y to love, _____ love, _____ love. _____

Find me some - bod - y to love, _____ find me some -

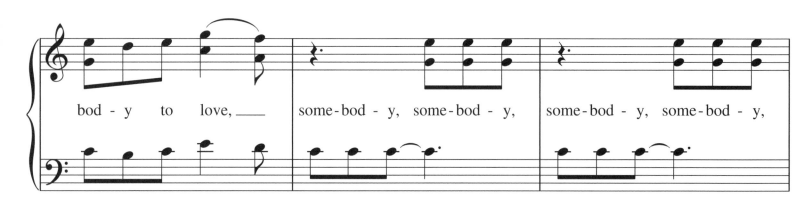

bod - y to love, ___ some-bod - y, some-bod - y, some-bod - y, some-bod - y,

some-bod - y. Find me some-bod - y, find me some - bod - y to love. Can

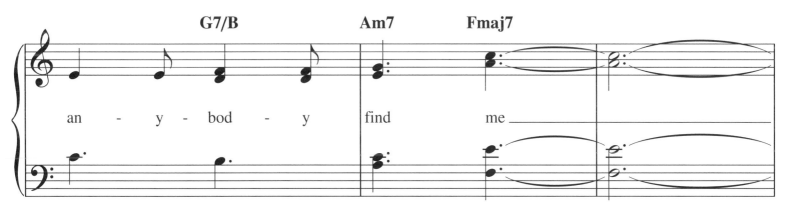

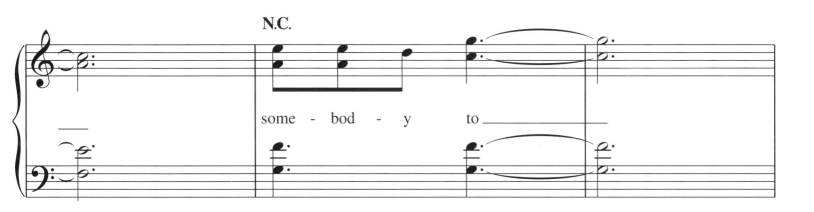

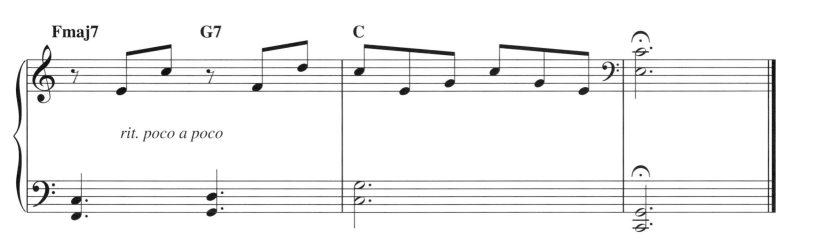

# SWEET CAROLINE

Words and Music by
NEIL DIAMOND

**Moderately, very steady**

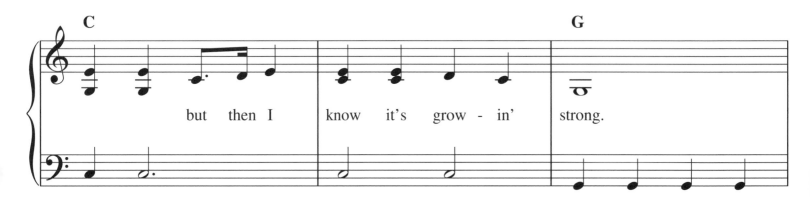

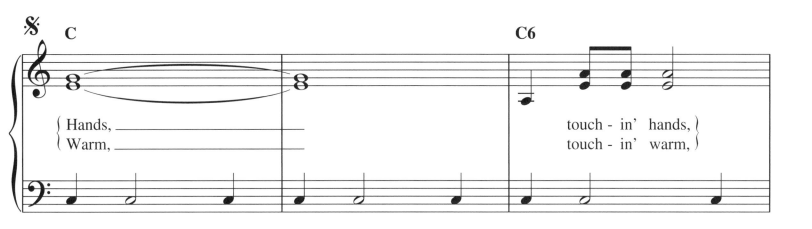

reach-in' out,        touch-in' me, _____

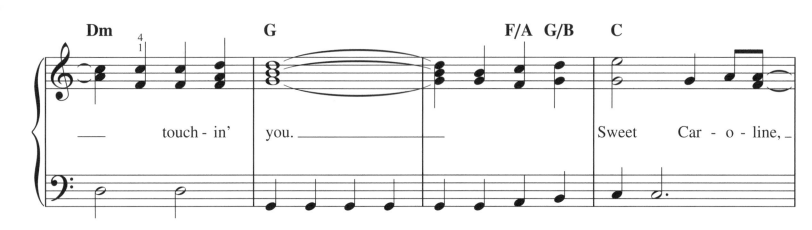

_____ touch - in' you. _____       Sweet    Car - o - line, _

_____             good times nev - er seemed so

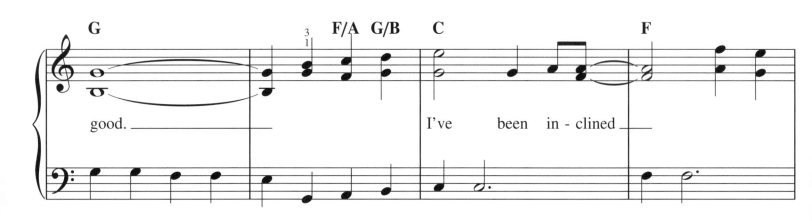

good. _____       I've been in - clined _____

to be - lieve ___ they nev - er would. { But  
                                        { Oh,

now         I }  
no,     I,  no. }         look   at   the   night,

and   it don't   seem   so   lone - ly.         We   fill   it

up   with   on - ly   two.                         And when I

hurt,  hurt - in' runs  off  my  shoul - ders.

How  can  I  hurt  when  hold - in'  you?

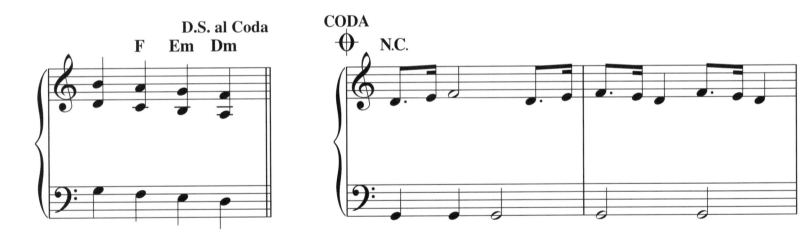

Sweet Car - o - line, \_\_\_ good times nev -

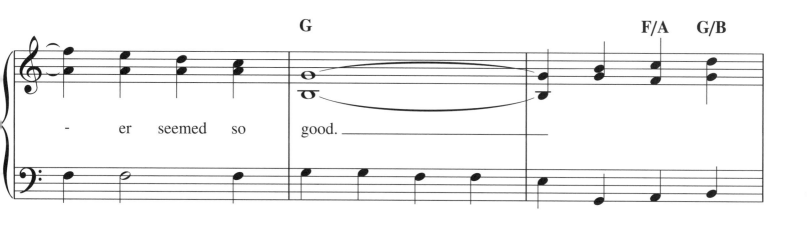

- er seemed so good. \_\_\_

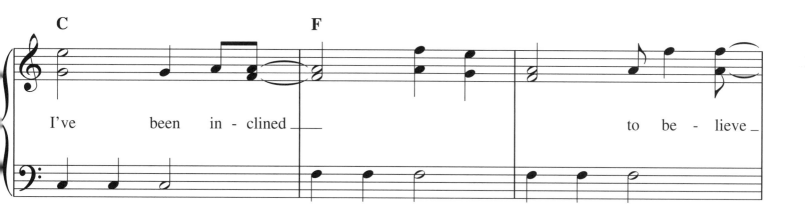

I've been in - clined \_\_\_ to be - lieve \_

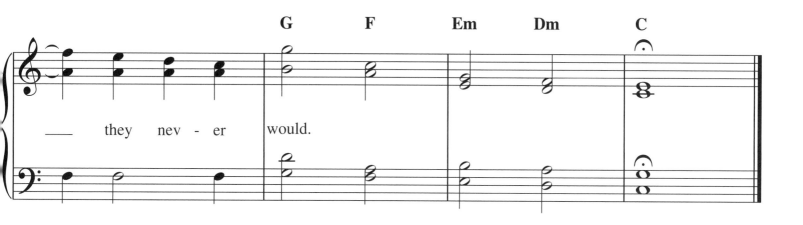

\_\_ they nev - er would.

# TRUE COLORS

Words and Music by BILLY STEINBERG
and TOM KELLY

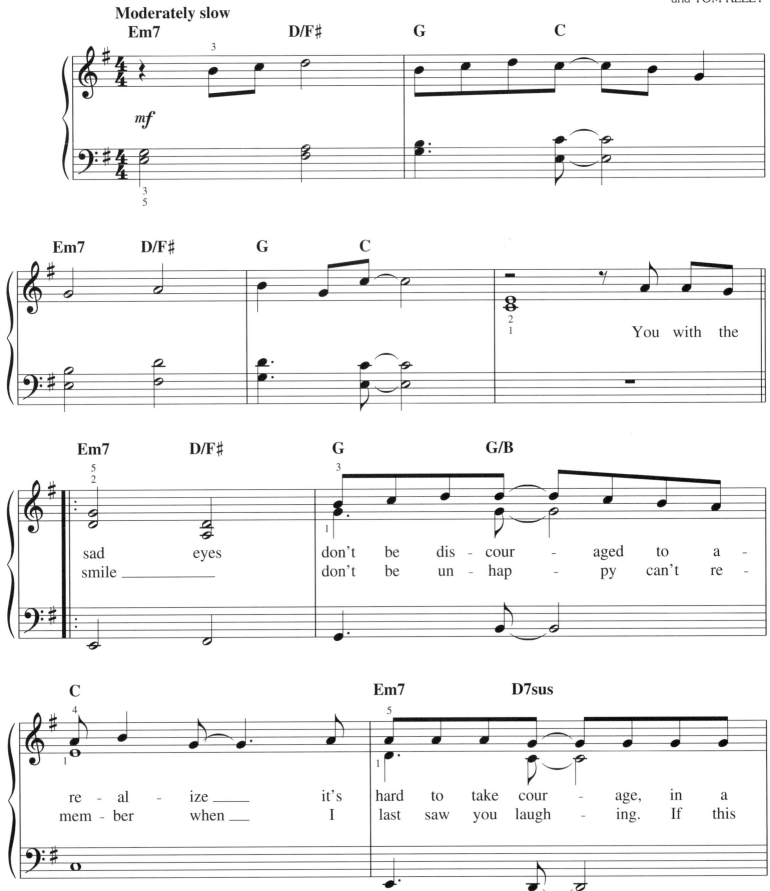

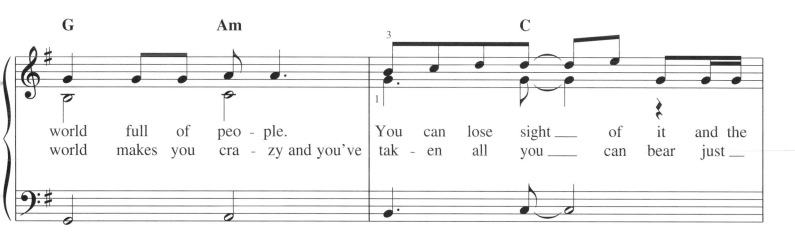

world     full     of     peo - ple.     You can lose sight __ of it and the
world makes you cra - zy and you've tak - en all you __ can bear just __

dark - ness     in - side     you makes you     feel     so     small. __ But I see your
call me     up     be - cause you     know I'll be     there. __ And I see your

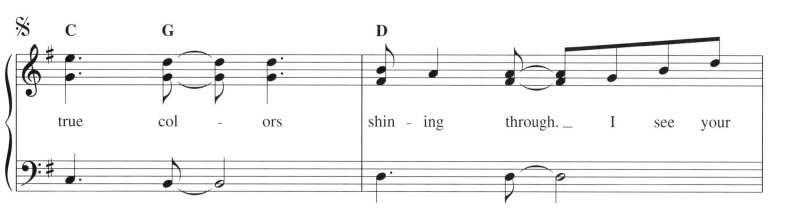

true     col - ors       shin - ing     through. __ I see your

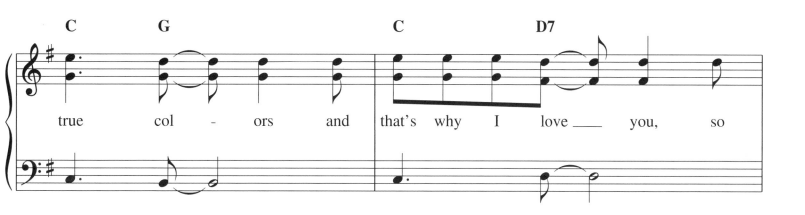

true     col - ors     and     that's why I love __ you, so

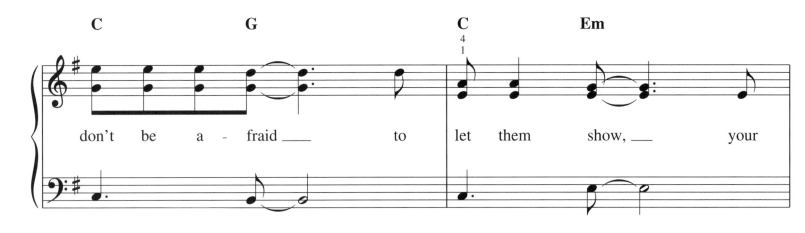

don't be a - fraid \_\_\_\_ to let them show, \_\_\_ your

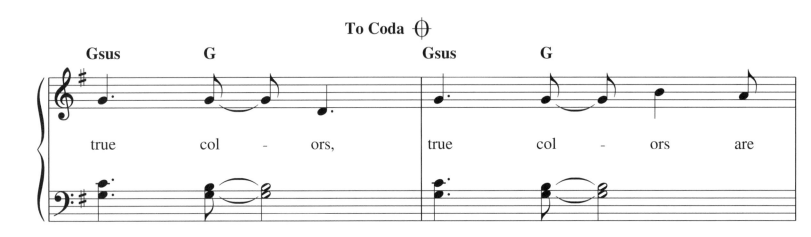

true col - ors, true col - ors are

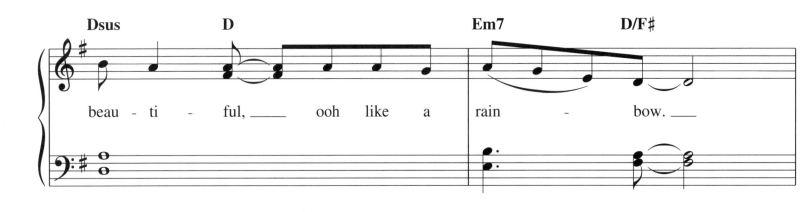

beau - ti - ful, \_\_\_\_ ooh like a rain - bow. \_\_\_

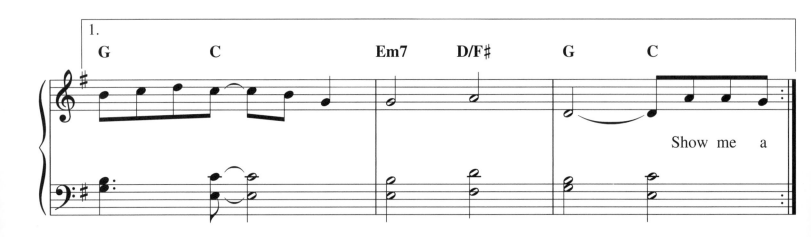

Show me a

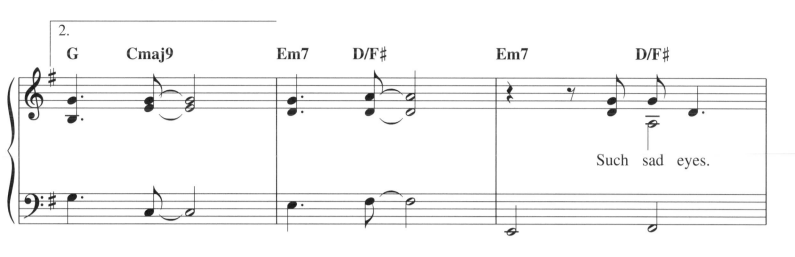

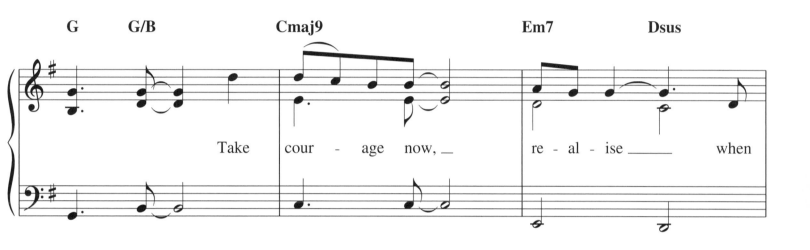

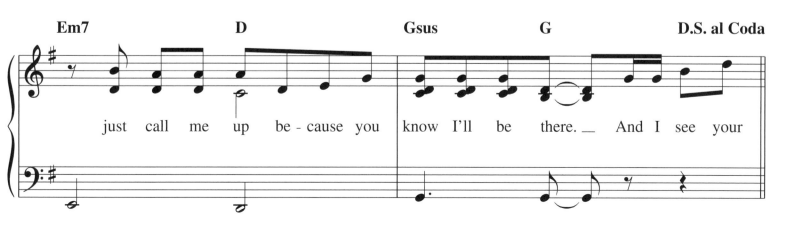

**CODA**

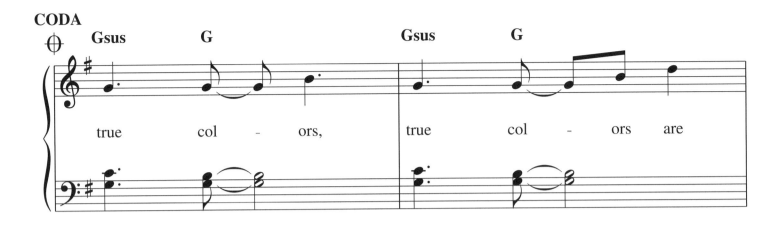

true col - ors, true col - ors are

shin - ing through. __ I see your true col - ors and

that's why I love __ you, so don't be a - fraid __ just

let __ them show, __ your true col - ors,

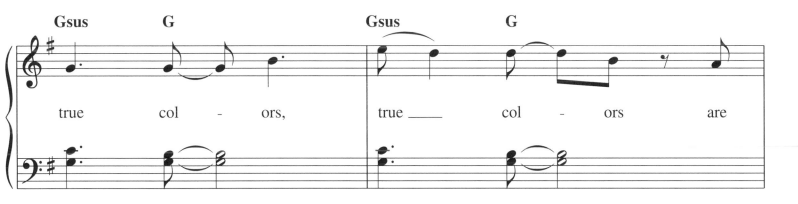

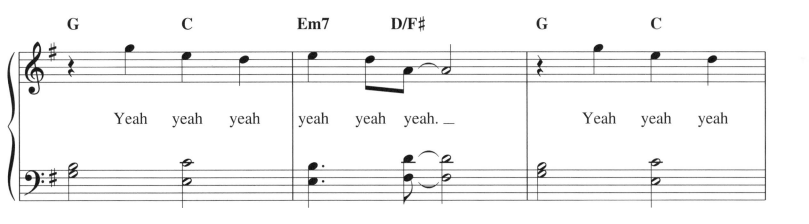

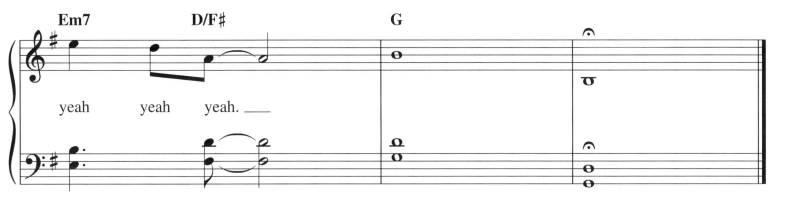

# TAKING CHANCES

Words and Music by DAVE STEWART
and KARA DioGUARDI

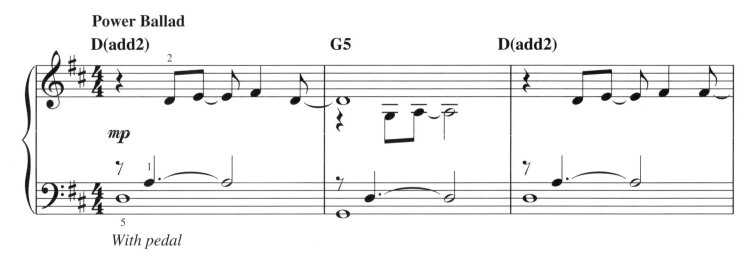

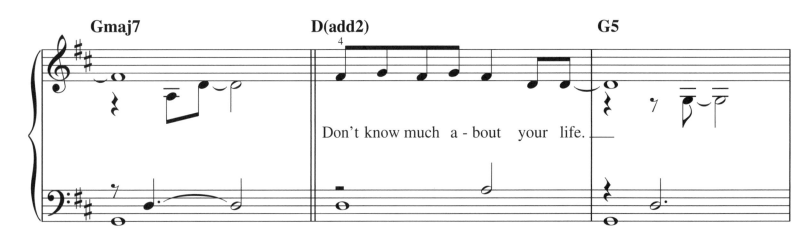

Don't know much a-bout your life.

Don't know much a-bout your world, ___ but, ___ don't wan-na be a-lone to-night,

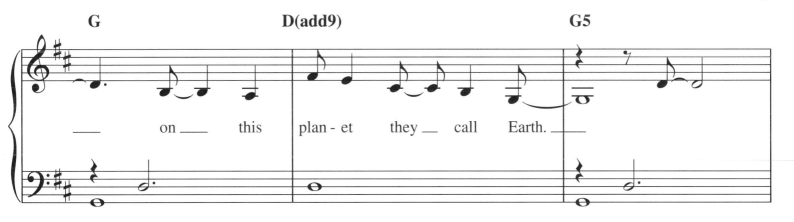

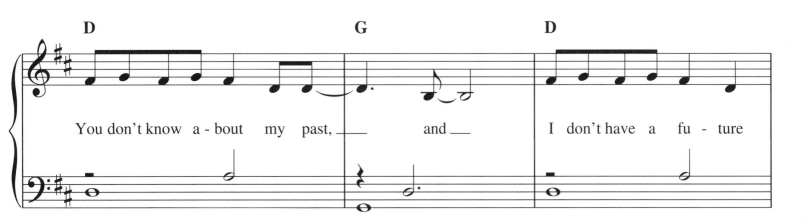

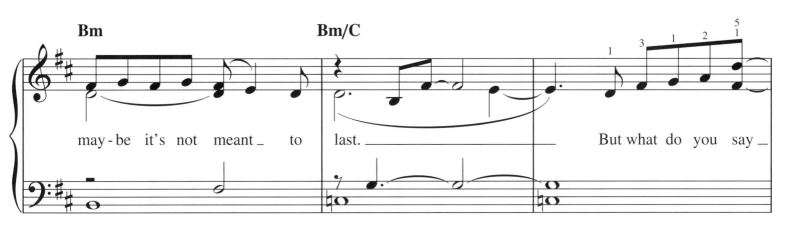

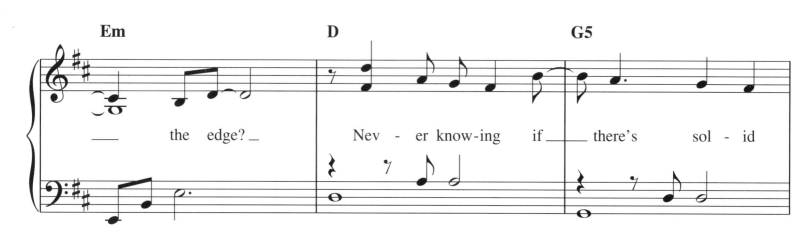

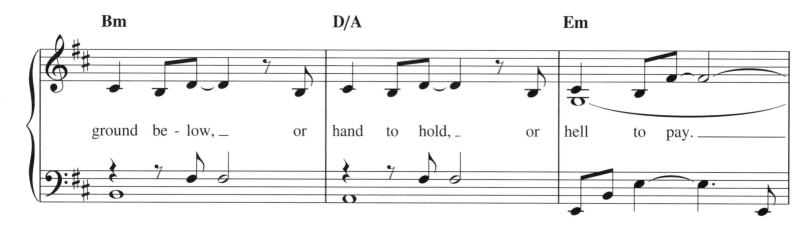

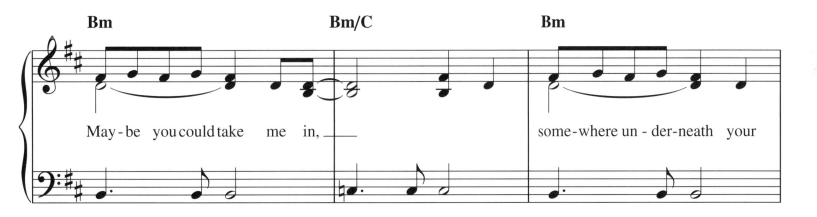

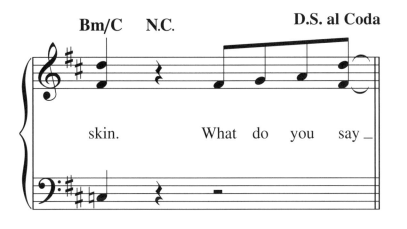

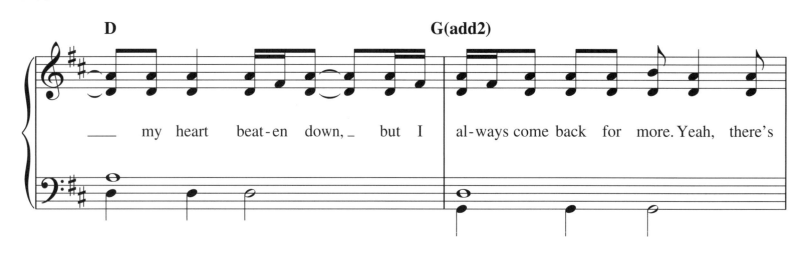

**D**       **G(add2)**

_____ my heart beat-en down, _ but I | al-ways come back for more. Yeah, there's

**D**       **G(add2)**

noth-in' like love to pull you up ____ when you're | lay-in' down on the floor there. So

**D5**       **G5**

talk to me, ___ talk to me like | lov-ers do. Yeah,

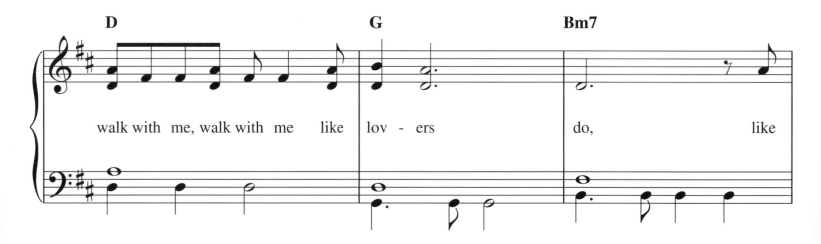

**D**    **G**    **Bm7**

walk with me, walk with me like | lov-ers do, like

lov - ers _____ do. _____ What do you say _

_____ to tak - ing chanc - ces? What do you say ____ to jump - ing off _

_____ the edge? _ Nev - er know ing if _____ there's sol - id

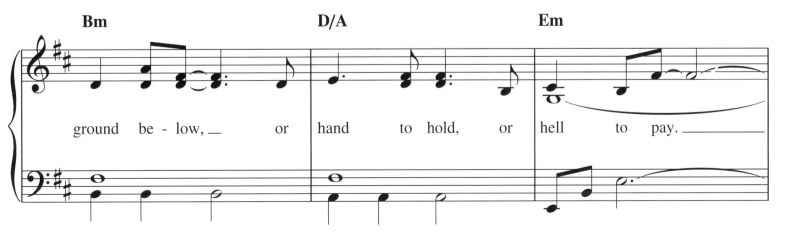

ground be - low, _ or hand to hold, or hell to pay. _____

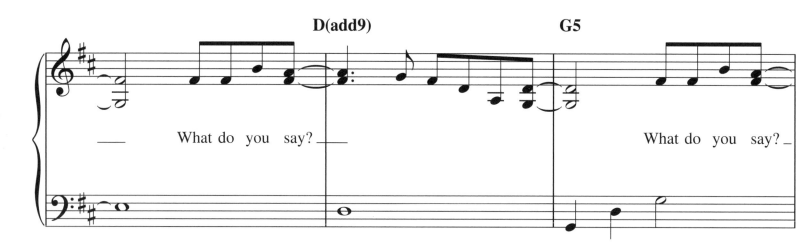

What do you say? ___      What do you say? ___

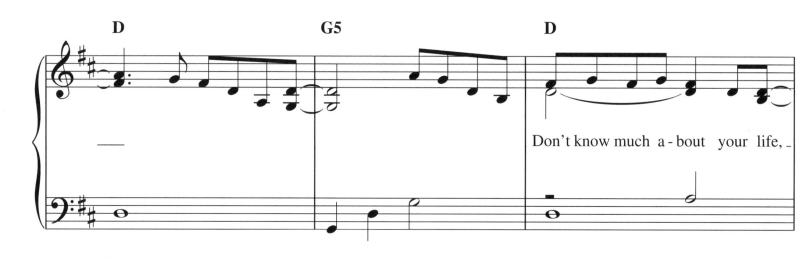

___      Don't know much a-bout your life, ___

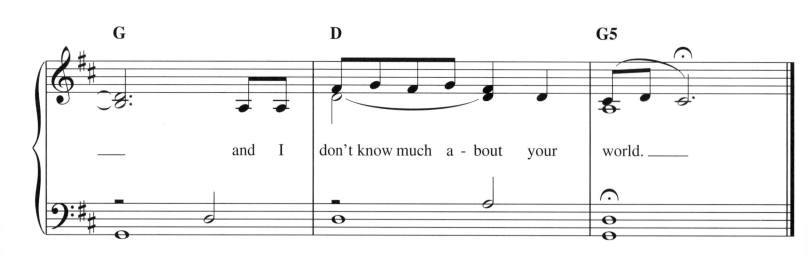

___     and I    don't know much a-bout your    world. ____